This book belongs to:

____

(1) Marah Roberson

Manufactured by Amazon.ca
Bolton, ON

21012437R00061